THE FALSE PROMISE OF DISCIPLESHIP

Rescuing Discipleship from the American Gospel by Asking the Right Questions

BILL HULL AND BRANDON COOK
FOREWORD BY BOBBY HARRINGTON

The False Promise of Discipleship
Copyright © 2019 Bill Hull and Brandon Cook

Requests for information should be sent via email to HIM Publications. Visit www.himpublications.com for contact information.

Any Internet addresses (websites, blogs, etc.) in this book are offered as a resource. They are not intended in any way to be or imply an endorsement by HIM Publications, nor does HIM Publications vouch for the content of these sites for the life of this book.

All rights reserved. No part of this book, including icons and images, may be reproduced in any manner without prior written permission from copyright holder, except where noted in the text and in the case of brief quotations embodied in critical articles and reviews.

Unless otherwise indicated, all Scripture quotations are taken from the Holy Bible, New Living Translation, copyright © 1996, 2004, 2007 by Tyndale House Foundation. Used by permission of Tyndale House Publishers, Inc., Carol Stream, Illinois 60188. All rights reserved.

Scriptures marked ESV are taken from The Holy Bible, English Standard Version® (ESV®), copyright © 2001 by Crossway, a publishing ministry of Good News Publishers.

All rights reserved.

All emphases in Scripture quotations have been added by the authors.

ISBN 978-1-970102-03-1 (paperback)
ISBN 978-1-970102-21-5 (Kindle)
ISBN 978-1-970102-22-2 (ePub)

Cover and interior design: Harrington Interactive Media

CONTENTS

Foreword *by Bobby Harrington* 5

1 | Our Way vs. Jesus' Way of Making Disciples
Introducing the False Promise 7

2 | The Human Paradigm
How Our Foundation Needs to Be Fixed 17

3 | The Failure of The Human Paradigm
Why Discipleship Efforts So Often Get Stuck 29

4 | The Jesus Paradigm
Reorienting Our Lives Around the Right Questions 39

5 | The Place of Obedience
Learning to Live into the Third Question 49

Notes 69

About the Authors 71

FOREWORD

Bill Hull is one of the best discipleship leaders writing today. Together with the deep thinking of Brandon Cook, the two leaders show us how to love Jesus, love Jesus' kingdom mission (to make disciples), love the church, and love the world. They will help you to do the same.

The False Promise of Discipleship will draw you into the heart of Jesus and compel you to ask the right question. It is the most fundamental question that should be asked about the focus and goal of discipleship. Hint: This question is not about you, and it's not about you and God.

Hull and Cook deftly raise *the issue* that church leaders need to grapple with today (and in all generations). This issue should form a seamless bridge between the best of the discipleship movement and the best of the missional movement. In fact, properly understood, it points us to a merger of the discipleship movement and the missional movement.

As soon as I read this book, I thought to myself: *I want my staff in our church and my national discipleship leader friends to read this book!* Then I thought to myself again, *Wait, a lot of other young leaders in their 20s and 30s out there really need this book.* Then I smiled when I said to myself, *I think God will be very pleased if a lot of people read* The False Promise of Discipleship, *and God will be especially pleased if they put what they read into practice.*

—Bobby Harrington, Co-founder and Executive Director of Discipleship.org and Renew.org; co-author of *DiscipleShift* and *The Disciple Maker's Handbook*

1

OUR WAY VS. JESUS' WAY OF MAKING DISCIPLES

Introducing the False Promise

> *"I hurt with the hurt of my people. I mourn and am overcome with grief. Is there no medicine in Gilead? Is there no physician there? Why is there no healing for the wounds of my people?"*
> —Jeremiah 8:21-22

Imagine if Jesus had spent all of his time planning a big banquet. He gets baptized in the Jordan River and then retreats back up to Galilee, puts a deposit down on a huge venue, and prepares to put on a killer party. No need for deejays to get the party started. The man makes a world-class wine.

Then the big night comes, and Jesus waits: eager, excited, his foot tapping nervously on the floor. But by 8 p.m., only a few people have shown up. He makes do. At least the sparse crowd enjoyed the wine (*what on earth* was *that vintage?*). The next week, Jesus tries the whole thing again, hoping for a better turnout. This time he brings in a band. But once again, the numbers are low.

Not one to give up, he tries it again, adding dry ice and a fog machine (the ancient equivalent, anyway). He continues to attempt a bigger and better party.

Kind of a crazy scenario, right? But when you think about it, for the last 50 years, the American church has been doing the same thing, with fewer and fewer people showing up for the party. Even when attracting people *has* worked to bring people to a local church, we haven't consistently created Christlike disciples and disciple makers. The harder we try, the further behind we get. The cultural landscape is shifting so rapidly and substantially that the strategies are outdated before we even get out of the gate. Trying to build church programs and having a slick show may still "work" in some parts of the United States, but increasingly, the impact of the attractional model is more like, "Turn out the lights; the party's over."

Bottom line: *The church as we've known it is dying. What will be resurrected in its place?*

We Need a New Movement

Of course, we know that Jesus did *not* focus on putting on a slick, attractive show.

He didn't throw a big party (although he did crash a few). Instead, he spent the vast majority of his time with a few individuals. Looking at his life in the Gospels, we can clearly see that Jesus zeroed in on making disciples, not on throwing parties. We can all give thanks for the growing awareness and conviction that disciple-making—following Jesus and learning to live and love like Jesus—is our work too. *Disciple-making is the hope for the church's future.* As author and 3DM leader Mike Breen has said, "If you make disciples, you will always get the church, but if you make the church, you won't always get disciples."[1]

In Luke's Gospel, we read Jesus' words to the crowd that had gathered: "If any of you wants to be my follower, you must give up your own way, take up your cross daily, and follow me. If you try to hang on to your life, you will lose it. But if you give up your life for my sake, you will save it" (Luke 9:23-25).

When we follow his plan, everything gets done just right. We can all greet the discipleship renaissance with hope. It is a breath of fresh air. It is a commitment that teems with possibilities.

Yet at the same time, *we are writing this book because we have major problems with discipleship—at least as we understand it.*

I (Brandon) grew up in the church and walked through a string of discipleship programs. Usually, they involved reading the Bible and talking about whatever I (or we, depending on who was in the group) was struggling with. The assumption seemed to be that if we just read more and tried harder, we could get ourselves in order and live real, effective lives for Jesus. There was value in that thought, for sure. But I always left each program with the feeling that I wasn't quite "there," that I simply needed to try harder, that there was some special place of arrival just around the corner if I did things the right way.

Ultimately, I ended up resenting the entire process because I could never get "there." I've discovered that most people approach God the same way, thinking that all they need to do is earn their way toward him, and then they end up frustrated by the entire process. Sure, everyone talks about grace when it comes to getting our sins forgiven and going to heaven, but almost immediately we separate that grace from the rest of our lives and start striving on our own to get to a new level with God. I've watched many of my peers leave the church entirely.

What's happening? Bill and I believe we're losing a generation because, at the root, *we've not taught discipleship as Jesus taught it.*

In fact, for many people these days, committing to "discipleship" may not actually mean much. The word has so many meanings—much like the word "Christian" (just notice how *that* word is wielded in media and popular use). We can't assume we know what any one person means when they say discipleship. As I (Bill) often say, we may be using the same words, but we are speaking a different language.

Is discipleship mentoring? Is it meeting regularly with someone or with a few someones? Maybe, maybe not. It all depends on what's happening (the content) during that time. Discipleship probably *includes* mentoring, but mentoring is not sufficient in and of itself to constitute discipleship. Or is discipleship teaching people to read Scripture and to talk about what they're struggling with? That is, is it Bible reading with some accountability thrown in?

Again, discipleship no doubt includes Scripture reading as well as honestly sharing our lives with one another. But is that how Jesus spent all of his time with the disciples—reading Scripture and asking them to tell him what they struggled with during the past week? Clearly, we don't have a lot of clarity about what discipleship is (and isn't). Moreover, our ways and means of making disciples may have little resemblance to how Jesus made disciples. To some degree, it makes sense—given we live in a completely different context absent of itinerant teachers who travel the countryside. And yet, *might there be something fundamentally askew about our baseline assumptions of what discipleship is?* Our problems, after all, aren't usually caused by what we know but just the opposite: what we *don't know*.

This book examines why discipleship, so called, so often fails and to explore what's required to restore potency and power to discipleship within our churches. Ultimately, it's about what we need to do in order to see towns and cities renewed, and the world to find hope in the living God.

It's like building and moving into a new house. You lay the foundation first, clearing away rubble, making a sure start. Then you raise the actual structure. It takes a lot of work, but oh boy, when you're done, holy Toledo! A veritable castle. You move in, excited for a new beginning. But over time, you notice that something's wrong. Your glass of orange juice starts sliding across the kitchen table. One day you notice that the living room floor dips in the middle. The corners of the bedroom are no longer flush. The siding is askew.

Naturally, you call in a carpenter, and then an engineer, eager to learn what has gone wrong. You soon discover the problem, and it's a doozy: you've built the entire structure on a rotten foundation. You think back, and truth be told, you *do* remember wondering if everything had been made level, if everything had been allowed to settle. But you were just so excited to get on with it and build the house. The extra work seemed like a waste of time. *Everything would probably be fine.* Or so you thought. Now, as you look at your house, which is quickly losing integrity, you realize that you'll either need to put some major work into overhauling and rehabbing the whole thing, or you'll just have to start from scratch, razing everything down to the foundation and beginning again.

Is it possible that our foundation for discipleship could be wonky? Is it possible that it might be off in some way, perhaps significantly? Jesus warned us, after all, about building our house on sand rather than on rock (Matt. 7:24-27). Of course, he was talking about building a life on him, but the metaphor holds true for whatever endeavor we set our hearts and hands to.

Could it be that too often we've built our discipleship on sandy beaches?

The False Promise

The false promise of discipleship deals with the premise that *discipleship is about a disciple getting closer and closer to Jesus.* The false promise of discipleship, simply, is the belief that discipleship is about ascending a ladder to get close to God.

Isn't being close to Jesus a great thing? Of course, it is! But here's the rub: a close relationship with Jesus is not the *end goal of discipleship.* Most people, quite simply, have been trained to think that discipleship is "for me":

- *It's about* me *growing closer to Jesus.*
- *It's about* me *becoming a better person and a better Christian.*
- *It's about* me *feeling like I know God more.*

All of these things are good. But this type of self-focused discipleship is exactly what has to shift. This myopic view is why maturity—which isn't even the type of maturity that Jesus desires for us—never happens. Whatever the paradigm for discipleship, if it's primarily about you and it's primarily asking the question, "How am I doing?" it's doomed to fall back to earth. We're left staring up at the heavens, knowing that surely there is soaring yet to be done but not quite sure how to get there above the clouds.

The soaring life that Jesus invites us into is, quite simply, *a life lived for others*. Contrary to what we've been taught or may have taught (or are currently teaching), discipleship is always, unceasingly about loving "the other"—which is God and other people. But in our discipleship efforts today, we've often stopped short of this. Being close to Jesus is part of the journey but not the only end goal. As God himself said to his people in Isaiah 58 (summarizing in our own words here): *If you'll focus on others, if you'll focus on rebuilding the broken places for others, if you'll focus on bringing light into the darkness, for others, then your salvation will break forth like the dawn!*[2]

Wasn't this Jesus' constant work? To provoke his disciples into loving and serving others, since he himself came "not to be served but to serve" (Mark 10:45)? Before Jesus fed the 5,000, he turned to his disciples and said, "*You* give them something to eat" (Matt. 14:16, ESV). He constantly challenged his disciples to love, serve, feed, and proclaim life to others. He said that the whole law and prophets—the whole story of God!—is about loving God with everything you have *and "your neighbor as yourself"* (Matt. 22:39).

Don't miss this: *Reorienting your life to loving, knowing, and serving others is both the heart of true discipleship and also the endpoint of discipleship.*

Yet, sadly, the church has not often adopted Jesus' ways and means toward this end—teaching his disciples to orient their life and energy around serving others. When it has, it feels more like an activity we're supposed to fit into crowded schedules rather than a lifestyle of adventure, teeming with possibilities, where the kingdom of God could burst forth at any moment. Sadly, we have often preferred to put on banquets, hoping people will like us, or outreach events, hoping that they will be curious about us. Good intentions, no doubt. But events and programs are simply not the path that leads to cultivating a vibrant church built on a movement of disciple-making disciples.

Through the course of this short book, we discuss specific steps toward a Jesus-centered, others-focused discipleship. But first, we need to explore why discipleship as it now stands—generally built on the question, "How am I doing?"—is so prevalent, and why true, Jesus-centered discipleship is often so elusive.

As with the call to the carpenter and the engineer, maybe we first need to put on our hard hats and take a good look at our foundations for life.

2

THE HUMAN PARADIGM
How Our Foundation Needs to Be Fixed

In John 3, we read the conversation between Jesus and Nicodemus, a leading Jewish figure. Nicodemus comes to Jesus under the cover of night, apparently worried about who might see him talking with the enigmatic rabbi from Galilee. He comes because he's concerned. He's wondering what foundation he's building his life on and if there's something he might be missing. After all, this teacher named Jesus speaks with an authority that Nicodemus has never before heard. Still, Nicodemus is conflicted: Jesus' message is compelling, but Nicodemus has built his life on a certain way of thinking about God and how one rightly approaches him. Namely, through the right sort of religious life—what Nicodemus uses to make himself acceptable before God.

Jesus says something quite strange that goes right over Nicodemus' head (summarizing in our own words):

Nicodemus, you must be born again.

Sure. Wait . . . what?

Jesus repeats it: "You must be born again," implying that Nicodemus must forsake what he was born into (his physical birth) and leave that behind to be born into something new (3:7).

Nicodemus is right in the thick of what he has been born into. Let's call it "The Human Paradigm," for it represents the paradigm of human life outside the kingdom of God.

What's Wrong with The Human Paradigm?

The Human Paradigm is endemic to most religious systems and beyond that to the human heart, where it gets its start. It's based on the idea that if we do A, B, and C, we can earn X—like a formula. (If you're having a cold-sweat flashback to sophomore algebra, fear not. That's as complicated as this equation gets.) This is like the "eat what you kill" paradigm that all of us are born into and grow up in, reinforced at every corner: "Be a good boy, and Santa will bring you lots of presents"; "Be a good girl, and Mommy will give you a cookie."

In The Human Paradigm, there's always some "X" that we want: presents, cookies, love and affection, etc. X marks the spot. It's the treasure we're after. We all have these Xs that we long for, and pretty much every human context has some X—the place we want to be. Advertisers are always preying on our belief that if we just have X or buy X, or take a vacation to X, we'll be finally satisfied. X might also represent what you want your life to be: having enough money, the house, the car, the boyfriend or girlfriend you're pining for, the skinny body you hope for. It's the place where people like you, or where you're confident. In short, it's the place where you've *arrived*. And won't life just be wonderful once you've arrived!

In the American mindset, it's all within your power—just follow the simple steps, whatever they may be. Consider this equation:

Or here's another popular one:

To make it more complicated, we tend to confuse these things we want with God's goal for our life. This creates the "American gospel," where we think the gospel is simply about the forgiveness of our sins so we can get into heaven while we pursue a life of individual freedom and prosperity. The message is like this: "God gives you what you want (heaven), if you give him what he wants (confession, conversion, etc.), and there's little other claim on your life to actually follow him." This is the consumer message at the heart of the American gospel. And tragically, we have exported the American gospel around the world.

What are your equations? What are the Xs in your life?

The two simple pictures below further illustrate The Human Paradigm:

There you are! And you're running! In The Human Paradigm, you're *always* running. You're always trying to arrive at the ever-elusive X.

But how? How do you get there? No problem. Just climb the right stairs. It's as easy as one, two, three . . .

So there are Xs, and then there are the steps we're supposed to take to get to X, the rungs we're to climb. If you just work hard, study, play nice, cheat, don't cheat, follow the rules, don't follow the rules, etc., you'll get to X! This is the heart of The Human Paradigm: do the things you're supposed to do, work hard enough, try hard enough, and you can get to X or make X happen. This paradigm is incredibly alluring because it promises us control. It's based on the governing narrative of the human universe that says if you try hard, you'll be rewarded. You are the master of your fate! The size of the self-help section in your local bookstore is a testimony to just how alive and well this paradigm of the American gospel is.

We were born into this way of thinking, and it's fine and good (to an extent) to rely on this paradigm. It reflects an actual reality of how the universe works. Right now, my wife and I (Brandon) are potty-training our daughter, and you better believe we're using such a system. Every time our little girl uses the potty, she gets gummy bears! Her X is gummy bears, and our X is getting our daughter to put her stuff where it's supposed to go so that (thank God) we don't have to change any more diapers. If we have to spend a small fortune on candy, so be it. Whatever works! We're using The Human Paradigm as a reward system to get something done. In this way, earning things we want works and is useful, insofar as we understand what we're doing. For some things in life, what you put into it, you get out of it.

But this paradigm is extremely limited in terms of how we approach God.

The flip side of The Human Paradigm—of earning what you get—is that if you do bad things, bad things will happen to you, either because the universe is karmic or because God will get you. You often find this thinking in religious circles. Jesus' disciples seem to fully depend on this sort of universe and on that sort of equation when they pass by the blind man and ask Jesus, "Rabbi, why was this man born blind? Was it because of his own sins or his parents' sins?" (John 9:2). (It's worth noting that Jesus doesn't buy into this way of thinking, answering, "Neither.") They were stuck in The Human Paradigm, which doesn't make room for The Jesus Paradigm.

The Human Paradigm is so prevalent because, quite simply, we really like it. We resent it when our equations don't work out. There's something alluring about the possibility that *if we do these things, we'll make it, we'll earn it, we'll arrive!* And we'll have done it all by ourselves.

Again, this sort of thinking is very much at home in most religious settings, and it translates quite easily into Christian spirituality. In the church world, the X may be a great thing, like being a good Christian, being the Christian I *should be*, being more giving, being missional, being more Spirit-filled (note: "should" is a huge word in The Human Paradigm). X represents the place where we have arrived at some point of envisioned spiritual maturity. And arriving at X is thought of as "being close to God."

Can you see the picture of arrival in your own faith? The place where you're no longer struggling with Y or Z because you've arrived at X? What would be complete in your personal realm of X? What struggles would you no longer have? And again, won't it just be wonderful when you get there!

What The Human Paradigm Is All About

When I (Bill) was nine years old, I went to the altar at my grandmother's church. A gaggle of praying folks surrounded me and informed me that I had "prayed through," which meant that I had been saved from my sins and was heaven-bound. Later that week, my grandmother informed me that I would need to be faithful and sometime in the next year or so, I would need to be sanctified. She said that was the next step. It was my X. A week later, I was laughing at my friends' off-color stories and thinking way too much about girls. I was moving in reverse. I never made it to X. Actually, X didn't look that good to me, but I knew I should try to get there, whether I liked it or not.

The big question, of course, is how do we get to X? Most church teaching offers up the answers in the form of a list of dos and don'ts, all designed to get us "close to Jesus." You just climb the rungs. If you do these things, you'll get to X.

Most church activity is based on the assumption that you're not close to Jesus and it's simply up to us to pull up our bootstraps and get close to him. You should do the things your church or denomination or tradition says you should do—go to church enough, read your Bible enough, get enough information in your head, pray enough, have enough faith, have enough quiet times, tithe enough, don't use those words, don't watch those movies—and you'll get to X.

The promise that we so often hear (and perhaps even teach), even if it's never explicitly stated, is that if you engage in certain religious practices in the right context—like through church membership or participation—you will become a mature Christian. Obviously, the rungs of this ladder vary according to context. In some legalistic contexts, a rung might be, "Don't cut your hair or wear shorts." In some holiness contexts, a rung might be, "Don't drink any alcohol." In other contexts, there's a way you're supposed to look or behave. Whatever the case, every context generally has a clear list of "shoulds" presented to us—things that we're supposed to do that will get us to X.

I (Brandon) have a very clear memory from high school of lying on my bedroom floor with a yellow legal pad, onto which I frantically scribbled all the things I could identify about myself that needed to be fixed. It was a spiritual inventory of sorts. And there were a lot of things to write down. I was hyper aware of all that I judged as unacceptable—to myself and, no doubt, to God. *Stop wanting so many material things. Stop being jealous. Make more time for prayer and Bible study.* Do this, don't do that. The list went on and on.

After I'd gotten a page full of items, I sat in frustration, literally rapping my fists on the floor at just how overwhelming it all was. But I couldn't see any other way. I felt incapable of transforming myself, and yet the only possibility I saw was trying harder. The only economy I knew was one based on me doing well enough to earn rewards, in this case, from God himself by mechanical obedience to him.

That's a stark example, and almost cartoonish, but I would assert that most of us, deep inside, have some sort of remnant belief that this is exactly how the universe works and that God's favor must simply be earned not just for entry into heaven but also for living a full life on this earth. And the reason we practice spiritual disciplines is to climb the rungs of the ladder and get to X. *That* is what The Human Paradigm is all about.

You can probably tell we're about to tear apart The Human Paradigm, but first it bears repeating that the basic elements of this paradigm are true and helpful. It's the way the world functions, and when Jesus said, "be wise as serpents," clearly there's something to be said about understanding how the world works (Matt. 10:16, ESV). Moreover, most of the "must dos" listed above—reading the Bible, praying and living generously and so forth—are great things! And we do them to pursue God and seek from them some sort of spiritual growth and transformation. All of that is true.

That said, The Human Paradigm has some real problems. And many of us are stuck in life because we've bought into this paradigm, which results in a lot of confusion, frustration, and ultimately anger toward God. We get stuck there because while we understand how things work in the world, we don't understand how they work within God's kingdom, in which a totally different paradigm—an economy that is *not* based on earning—is the only economy that matters. So we need to understand the problems that come from The Human Paradigm because without understanding them, we will have a difficult time fully entering the kingdom of God and thriving as disciples of Jesus. To these issues we now turn.

3

THE FAILURE OF THE HUMAN PARADIGM
Why Discipleship Efforts So Often Get Stuck

The first, and perhaps the most obvious, problem with The Human Paradigm is that we never arrive! Have you noticed that X is ever-elusive? The closer you get to it, the farther away you realize it is. This plays out in life all the time, when say, we get the job we wanted and find that somehow it doesn't satisfy us. Have you ever noticed that getting what you thought you wanted can actually be a miserable experience?

And in spiritual terms, we all know that for all the growth and progress we make, there's always more to go. We're never where we could or "should" be. The more mature you get, the more you realize that attaining some sort of spiritual standing on your own merits is not going to happen. We're always discovering just how far we are from the person we want to be. And yet many—if not most—of us believe that we have to earn God's love or grace, and then resent that we aren't able to do it.

That's a real problem.

As much as we grow, we never arrive and we can feel like we're traveling in a circle and not in a straight line. For this reason, many Christians get burned out on following Jesus. It's just exhausting—if you're approaching it through The Human Paradigm.

Growing up, I (Brandon) was constantly told to have a quiet time for prayer and reading Scripture. I thought that was the only way I would get close to God. While I've come to learn the value of these disciplines, the way I understood it was:

It was an equation to me. When I practiced these, I did sense the value in quieting my soul. To this day, I believe that silence makes way for an encounter with God, and that without silence there is no space for spiritual transformation. Yet I struggled—as did most everyone else I knew—with having quiet times. It's just hard and somehow unnatural to approach with any eagerness a God who you believe, at root, is trying to fix you or trying to get you to climb a ladder toward him.

Many people, in fact, leave the church entirely after discovering that "doing the dance" doesn't deliver all they thought it would. They've mistaken the relationship for rules. People leave the church because they discover the gospel they have believed—that life will basically work out if you do this dance—proves to be insufficient. Tragedy occurs. Life twists and turns, sometimes painfully, and if you believe that it's because you didn't do the dance well enough, you'll either conclude that God is capricious or that all this Jesus stuff is just hooey. You think, *This just can't be who God is, and if it is, then I want no part of it.*

Who can blame you? You may have been taught, in essence, "do these things, and everything will be okay," instead of "everything will *not* always be okay, but God is with you and that's enough!" Our gospel, under the influence of The Human Paradigm, is often way off. Rather than teaching people the gospel of God already with us, we've taught them the gospel of "do it right to get close to Jesus."

How Am I Doing?

The second problem—and this is a critical one—is about focus. Where is the focus in this paradigm? On self! How am *I* doing? Am *I* having enough faith? Am *I* reading my Bible enough? I, I, I! In fact, as we said earlier, the defining question in The Human Paradigm is "How am *I* doing?"

Now, this is not a bad question per se. In fact, it's a great discipleship question that Jesus often uses. How you're doing matters—to an extent. But if that's your only, or even primary, discipleship question, you're in big trouble. Any spirituality exclusively, or even primarily, focused on this question is cut off from real life and vitality in Christ. It's trapped, imprisoned; it leads to highly educated Christians who have no real outlet for their knowledge and desire. They often grow tired and give up, and the desire for more dissipates into the tissue of ordinary life.

The problem is that while the question, "How am I doing?" is really satisfying to the ego, the concerns of our spirit are wholly different. We were designed to be most satisfied by forgetting ourselves, not by focusing on us. Heaven is a sort of self-forgetfulness. Jesus described our way of being "like little children" (Matt. 18:3). Think of the freedom of a two-year-old who has not yet developed their fear of "what people might think about me." That's part of what it means to be like little children in the kingdom.

Come over to my (Brandon's) house most nights and you'll find our daughter dancing in circles, the definition of "throw your hands in the air like you just don't care."

When we give to others, we become self-forgetful, which is not far from an experience of heaven. When we focus on others instead of our own immediate needs, when we do something beautiful for another, we discover that truly "it is more blessed to give than to receive" (Acts 20:35). And the opposite holds true: the heart of hell is a soul focused only on its self and its own needs at the expense of others. So it's very unlikely we will experience much joy or abundance if we're constantly monitoring, evaluating, and bemoaning on the one hand—or pridefully exulting, on the other—how poorly or how well we're doing.

Jesus is constantly trying to get our focus off of ourselves and onto loving God and loving others. He said that a life of loving and serving others is the mature result of his work in human hearts (Mark 10:45). But oftentimes, we are so caught in a paradigm that has trained us to constantly check in on how well we're doing at being "good Christians" that we never actually *become* good Christians.

Spiritual Practices Get Ruined

In The Human Paradigm, spiritual practices—reading Scripture, praying, fasting, and so forth—get ruined. They become about earning our way toward God rather than becoming aware of God. But we are transformed by becoming aware of who God is—his character, his nearness, his goodness. Paul described it as being transformed as we see and gaze upon God (2 Cor. 3:18). Spiritual practices are crucial to our development as disciples because they create space for this experience of God's goodness and encounter with it. But in The Human Paradigm, even if we exert effort to engage spiritual practices, it may not be the sort of effort that actually opens us to God. Sometimes people who engage spiritual practices, for example, try to get life to work on their own terms and control life. They might think, *If I just pray in exactly the right way, I can keep myself from suffering.* Engaging in spiritual practices as Jesus taught us to will lead us into an experience of vulnerability before God and a deep recognition of our need for him. This is how we become open to God so that we can be transformed.

The False Promise of Discipleship

The Biggest Problem

What we've mentioned so far are issues for sure, but the biggest problem with The Human Paradigm is just that: that The Human Paradigm is strictly human. It's a human way of thinking about the world. It is, at its core, untouched by the economy of God's kingdom. And, at its core, it is often driven by a misshapen view of God. *The gas that drives the entire engine is the belief that God must be persuaded that we are worthy of further good things and responsibility.* That we must wrestle blessings from his hand, that, ultimately . . . God is not really good and generous.

It's amazing when we start to discover just how deep that belief runs in us, even if we would never acknowledge it on an intellectual or theological level. But there is always the belief of the mind and the belief of the heart—what we *really* believe on an emotional level. There's the truth we ascribe to and the truth we actually hold to. It's amazing just how far our thoughts about God can be from reality.

As Dallas Willard said, most people are most comfortable thinking of God as an exterminator, a hammer in hand ready to smite us.[3]

A young woman in a Bible study once said to me (Brandon), "People keep telling me, 'God's your good father,' but that doesn't mean anything to me! I don't have warm and fuzzy thoughts when I think about *my own father*, and I don't have warm and fuzzy thoughts when I think about God as Father." This woman knew what she was *supposed to* believe about God, but what she actually believed, based on her experience with her earthly father, was something else entirely. Thank God she was in touch with her heart and honest enough to say so!

So let's add some images to The Human Paradigm. In the illustration below, God is either angry, ambivalent and distant, like an old Grandfather in the Sky, or is absent altogether.

Even if we have had amazing experiences with Jesus, an inner knowledge and intuition of who he really is, and a bunch of intellectual and theological training to back it up, we nevertheless often have remnant beliefs, deep down in our souls, that God is simply not that good. So we have to *do* good or make ourselves good so that he'll pay attention to us. We know this is bad theology, but the beliefs of the heart often outweigh the theology of the mind. The Bible has a word for images of God that we fashion and worship, trying to wrestle blessing from it: idols. And if you know Scripture, you know that 100 percent of the time idolatry leads to death.

In his conversation with the Jewish leader Nicodemus, recorded in John 3, Jesus was nudging him toward a confrontation with his view of God—a God he could wrestle blessing from by following all the rules. Like the older brother in the Parable of the Prodigal Son (Luke 15), Jesus tends to zero in on religious people who put their confidence and trust in their ability to be in the Father's house by "slaving" for the Father. The belief that we can earn it with brute effort, even if that's not what we *really* want, is such a powerful narcotic.

We want God—or so we say—but we also really want to avoid being undone by something that's beyond our ability to control, which makes grace, really and truly, a very difficult thing for us to receive. Humility is just as difficult.

Oftentimes, in the name of "discipleship," we've tried to get people to merely do better or simply try harder because that's what we do ourselves, driven by a warped view of God. Oftentimes, we believe more in The Human Paradigm than we do in the grace, nearness, and goodness of God. And if we live by The Human Paradigm, we entirely misread and completely misunderstand the story of the New Testament and what was accomplished in the life, death, and resurrection of Jesus Christ.

Jesus knows, as he tells Nicodemus, that we must be born again. We must die to our merely human ways of thinking and be born into the kingdom of God. For in Jesus' kingdom, things work very, very differently, and The Human Paradigm falls apart.

4

THE JESUS PARADIGM
Reorienting Our Lives Around the Right Questions

Rather than building on sand, the wise builder asks, "Hey, is there a rock around here?"

Jesus demolishes The Human Paradigm and replaces it with something wonderful and glorious, dazzling and brilliant. The Jesus Paradigm—which is life inside his kingdom—looks something like the the image to the side here.

X still marks the spot, but the X is territory claimed by the cross of Jesus. The difference is that there are no rungs because, in Jesus' view, *we are already "there."* "You're in," Jesus says. "It's done. You've been adopted."

ADOPTION!

It's unlike the economy of The Human Paradigm, where "you eat what you kill." Earning by human standards *does* work in our world exactly as described in The Human Paradigm. But grace!

Grace—which drives the kingdom of God—does not run on the gas of earning, competence, or merit. Grace stands in complete contrast to our merely human ways of doing things, which is why we call it amazing. We don't come by strength; we come by being weak and acknowledging that weakness. Paul said we rejoice in our weakness and rely on God's grace (2 Cor. 12:9).

We earn nothing; we just learn to abide. We become okay with *not* arriving. That's what abiding is all about: not arriving. Our labor is not to earn but to surrender to what Jesus has done. This is a sort of dying, what Jesus calls "being born again." He knows that trying really hard is actually not how spiritual growth happens. Transformation happens when we learn that our best efforts aren't going to get us there, and that God was never merely interested in our best efforts in the first place. It's the very reason Scripture tells us to "enter that rest" (Heb. 4:11).

What a paradox! Entering rest means coming into a completely new understanding of God's economy of grace. Going to conferences and reading books may be great things, but the reality is that the earliest disciples were not invited into seminaries or systematic theology classes or endless study. They were simply invited into a full awareness of who Jesus is and the Father whom Jesus reveals. If you're aware of this, if you become fully aware of just how good, generous, and near God is—then everything, yes *every thing*—will take care of itself. As we like to say, "Follow Jesus, and he will teach you everything you will ever need to know." Love takes care of it all. It's no wonder, then, that Jesus defines eternal life, very simply, as *knowing* the God of love (John 17:3). Not knowing *about* him but knowing him in the way you would know an intimate friend, a confidant, a spouse.

Our minds cannot readily grasp that God would so humble himself as to have mutuality and a reciprocal "knowing" in his relationship with us. But that's the very mutuality revealed in Immanuel, God with us. Further, Jesus so easily worked acts of power and grace because his feet were always rooted in the waters of the Jordan, even when they were dry: he always lived in that place where God said to him (again, our summary here of Matthew 3:17), *You are in. You are my beloved. I'm proud of you.* Jesus knew that he was "in," and because of that, he could bestow that "chosenness" on others. Everything good flows from knowing this "you're in" that God speaks over us. It's what Jesus came to adopt us into.

A disciple, then, is someone who, grounded by grace and guided by the Holy Spirit, is increasingly rooted in an understanding and experience of how generous God is—and how God has given us a new identity based not on our performance but on his profligately generous acceptance.

To be clear, this life grounded in grace is not a passive life. Scripture makes it clear that ours is a life of doing—indeed a life of great effort. Paul says, for example, that we will be judged by what we have done (Rom. 2:6). Before we are told to "enter that rest," we are told to "make every effort" to enter into this rest

(Heb. 4:11). We are told to "work out" our salvation (Phil. 2:12, ESV) and that we were created to do good things (Eph. 2:10). In fact, obedience is at the center of the Christian life (see John 14:15). As Dallas Willard famously said, "Grace is not opposed to effort; it's opposed to earning."[4] We put every effort into abiding in Christ. But the order is of utmost importance. We put in effort in response to what Christ has already completed. It's out of God's acceptance and his movement toward us that we act, do, and obey—not the other way around. We are accepted, adopted, and loved by God, and as a result, we love him through our actions with our entire being. This is a completely different orientation toward effort than one finds under The Human Paradigm.

God's grace doesn't make sense if we're used to The Human Paradigm. Everyone knows that Santa brings presents to only good boys and girls, and at a core level, most of us remain comfortable relating to Jesus like Santa Claus—a Santa Claus we can control. There's no space for thinking that we—broken, sinful, selfish people—could be adopted in and brought to the table, accepted. And it's this very unwillingness to receive that allows us to stay in control.

Like the tragic Inspector Javert in *Les Miserables*, throwing himself off a bridge because he can't accept the reality of grace, we have to wrestle with something that is completely offensive and insane to our merely human minds. This is why grace is so hard: it *is* an offense to our survival mechanisms and to every system of reward and punishment by which we've survived life. We are simply unready and untrained for grace. And so we drift back to The Human Paradigm and its mighty gravitational pull. We shrink the gospel to something with which we're more comfortable, something less offensive to our egos, something within our power to control. We reduce it down to the passive process of saying a prayer and waiting to go to heaven, rather than the process of fully entering, with great effort—indeed with our entire being—the transforming reality of grace that demands everything from us. As we like to say, grace costs us nothing, but it demands everything. That way, we're never confronted with the tension of needing to be humble enough to receive God's gift or to focus on the Giver rather than on ourselves.

I (Brandon) find that as much as I know about grace, there is some part of me—no doubt it's what the Bible calls my flesh or ego—that does *not* want to submit to God or even be touched by him. I'm always seeing how I can try to do the dance better, which must be more appealing to me than just saying, "Wow, I don't get it, but thank you!" I'm always thinking I can't approach Jesus if I'm not in a good space, if I've not been "doing well" (whatever I think that means). Again, where's the focus in that thinking? On me! Certainly not on God, and definitely not on others.

In short, if we live outside of The Jesus Paradigm, our energies will always drift back to focus, even obsession, on the question, "How am *I doing*?" But Jesus wants to redirect our energies. Of course, we get exhausted if our best discipleship processes are just rehashes of The Human Paradigm in the latest, hippest garb. This was never Jesus' intent for us. His goal was never to get us to try really hard to arrive—but that we should learn to abide. And from that abiding relationship learn how to reorient our lives around loving and serving others from a place of acceptance and not of earning to gain our acceptance. That commitment to reorientation of life and energy fuels our transformation into the image of Jesus.

The Beginning of New Questions

It takes practice to follow Jesus, and it takes practice and a whole lot of divine help and revelation to grow in grace.[5] But once we accept that we have been adopted into Christ, an amazing thing happens: we realize that "getting close to Jesus" is not the point of discipleship, and we shouldn't teach that it is. Jesus had a different end point in mind for his followers.

Once we accept the bankruptcy of The Human Paradigm and the reality that we will never "arrive," we can start asking new questions like, "God, how can you be this good?!" In the glory of God's goodness and generosity to us, our obsession with "How am I doing?" can melt away like wax. Indeed, it's only ever seeing the goodness of God that truly transforms us (2 Cor. 3:18).

And now we are prepared, simply by learning to receive what Jesus has done for us and others, to focus on the discipleship that Jesus taught. The end point of discipleship is not "getting close to Jesus." We are already close to him! Rather, the end point of discipleship is the result of being close to Jesus: loving God and others like we love our own self. And, ironically, almost like a cosmic joke, if we focus on loving others, our deepest spiritual needs and transformation seem to take care of themselves (see Isa. 58:8).

Without this focus on reorienting our life and energy around others, we don't experience true discipleship, the discipleship Jesus has for us. Once we start living in the question "How can you be this good, God?" it naturally follows that we ask the question, "How am I doing with loving others?" Love begets love, and love is self-forgetful. We don't have time to worry too much about ourselves because we're busy receiving and giving love. Receiving God's love begins to transform us into the sort of people who don't *try* to love our neighbors but who just do it naturally.

So discipleship movements must be built on these two questions:

> "God, how can you be this good?!"
>
> "How am I doing with loving others?"

These two questions form the basis of the whole point of the Law and Prophets, as Jesus teaches (see Matt. 12:30-31; 22:40). That is, they are the basis of God's work through human history and they are the questions into which Jesus would have us live.

The Promise of True Discipleship: A New End Point

Before we move on to the final chapter, let's pause to summarize the points we've covered:

1. *Reject the wrong question.* The Human Paradigm asks, *"How am I doing?"* This is not inherently a bad question, but if it's our primary discipleship question, then we're probably building discipleship on a false promise—a sandy foundation, so to speak. Discipleship that's focused on "getting closer to God" and "arriving" at some level of Christian performance is not what Jesus was about. The Human Paradigm overly focuses on "me," sacrificing true discipleship along the way. Discipleship borne out of The Human Paradigm will fail because it is a closed system that doesn't reproduce; it fails because no one ever arrives. In fact, striving through brute effort for a certain level of performance breeds self-contempt: the longer you try, the more you fail, and you know it. Usually, this leads to what Dallas Willard called "sin management."[6] Christianity becomes about trying to simply manage our most difficult sins until death, when Christ offers us victory. No wonder so many of our discipleship processes have no strength. They are built on the wrong question and the wrong assumption.
2. *Embrace the new question.* The Jesus Paradigm moves us into a new question: *"God, how can you be this good?!"* We are reoriented to a new reality in which the X we were striving for is, wonder of wonders, brought near to us! We are *al-*

ready there. We have to learn to abide in that reality, where the focus is not on ourselves and "how we are doing" but on the amazing goodness and nearness of Jesus. The reason for Christian practices or spiritual discipline is to develop your awareness of this gift of salvation. Asking the question—"God, how can you be this good?"—is a vast improvement and movement in the right direction. But left to its own devices, this wonderful question will also fail you.

3. ***Learn to appreciate God.*** God sure does appreciate our appreciating him (just as we love being appreciated by those we love), but it's not his end point for us. Appreciation and awe are always meant to lead us into obedience, into a new way of being people. God's mission for us, in short, is to become like him, which means learning to love and serve others with the same heart of authentic mercy, compassion, and love that he has. "Be perfect," Jesus said, "even as your Father in heaven is perfect" (Matt. 5:48). In his seminal work, *Mere Christianity,* C.S. Lewis writes, "The command, 'Be ye perfect' is not idealistic gas. Nor is it a command to do the impossible. He is going to make us into creatures that can obey that command."[7] "Being perfect" is an impossible task for us if we're resting on our effort alone. Yet Jesus will make us perfect if we will orient our lives around the third question.

4. ***Focus on loving others.*** The third question, which constitutes the heart of practical discipleship, is *"How am I doing with loving the people that God has already put in my life?"* Jesus was a man for others, and the church is really the church

when it exists for others. When we follow Christ, we live for others like Christ did.[8] Real discipleship—Jesus-style discipleship—has a very different end point than merely being close to him. If we're already close, then everything changes, and what is more, the goal of discipleship changes. What did Jesus define as the end point of discipleship? Very simply, loving others (Mark 12:30-31). Of course, we should expect nothing less from God, who is the very heart of love itself (1 John 4:8).

When we understand that loving others is at the heart of Jesus' method for training disciples, we can seek to catalyze movements of disciple-making that honor Jesus' own ways and means. In the next chapter, we'll explore the shape of movements that follow Jesus' way of teaching.

5

THE PLACE OF OBEDIENCE
Learning to Live into the Third Question

To learn to live into that third question of *"How am I doing with loving others?"* and to develop a movement of discipleship based on this question—that is the work ever-present before the church. It is the reason we cannot divorce discipleship from mission, as so often happens, as if they are two different things. The end point of a disciple-making movement, simply stated, is disciples who have reoriented their lives around loving God and others. We have to learn to live into this third question, and we have to learn to make disciples who do the same.

The urgent work of the church is to rescue discipleship from the clutches of The Human Paradigm. Notice how seldom discipleship in the church is intentionally oriented around loving others. Most of what we call "discipleship" is not Jesus-style discipleship. These discipleship programs, as such, fail because they're still built on the assumption that "getting close to Jesus" is our goal, our X, and that we can get close to Jesus, if we "just do these things."

If your goal as a church leader is to get people into a discipleship program that's founded on the question *"How are you doing?"* then you won't get mature disciples unless you're orienting them around receiving God's love and learning to love him, along with learning to love and serve others. We need a radical reorientation to our approach to discipleship. We have to start with the ending, as it were, and design discipleship processes that start with "you are already close to Jesus," which leads to loving others. In the middle of it all is the love of God.

And we have to design discipleship processes that compel people to reorient their lives around others as they are now, not waiting until they've arrived at some "ready point." That point will never come! We have to throw people into the deep end of the pool. After all, isn't that what Jesus did when he said to his disciples at the feeding of the 5,000, "*You* give them something to eat" (Matt. 14:16, ESV)? He taught them that everything he did was about loving God first and others second. This is our work too.

Healing Balm in Gilead?

The title of this book points out the emptiness of much of the discipleship in our churches, but at the same time, it's also meant to confess something. If there is a false promise, then there is a true promise as well—a healing "balm in Gilead" (Jer. 46:11, ESV). There is something real and genuine to be found in all this programming and infrastructure we call church that makes it all worthwhile. But we have to change our ways if we expect to find it.

I (Bill) recall the day that Brandon and I were discussing discipleship and this very matter of the third question came up: *How am I doing with loving the people whom God has already put in my life?* Brandon said that he often would struggle with conventional discipleship because it centered on getting people to do certain spiritual disciplines with no clear focus. The assumption was that transformation would simply result from doing these spiritual disciplines. Brandon asserted that these disciplines—praying, reading the Bible, fasting, silence and solitude, etc.—were falling flat because people were not arriving at X. I concur. The product of the church—our disciples—is not impressive. Moreover, they are not relevant to the world around us. I have always thought the church is for discipleship, and disciples are God's gift to the world. God has charged the church with the task of developing Christlike people, and then those people are sent back into the world to love like he loves.

At that point in the conversation, essentially, Brandon and I came up with the third question. Loving the people around us was the only relevant thing—a true expression of how God loves us.

Working This Out in Practical Terms

In his life, Dallas Willard spoke quite often of the "discipleship funnel," which is the idea that when you put all the discipleship teaching and tools from the church into the top of the funnel, the only worthwhile thing to come out from the bottom would be God's *agape* love. I (Bill) use the Greek word *agape* because of our tendency to misunderstand love primarily as an emotion or something romantic. *Agape* love, though, is an action taken for the benefit of another. This is where the third question comes into play: "How are we doing with loving the people in our homes, our workplace, our kids' schools and activities?" And we might also ask, "Who else is God bringing into my life for me to love?"

If discipleship looks like loving others, then how do we pursue it, practically speaking? In other words, how does all of this work out differently than the ways we have normally gone about discipleship? These are big implications that can't be covered in any depth in this short book, but we would like to suggest practical steps forward. We need to shift:

1. How we teach spiritual disciplines and practices,
2. How we approach corporate church services and gatherings,
3. How we think about and celebrate "mission,"
4. How we teach evangelism, and
5. How we lead discipleship groups.

Let's look at these five areas in brief:

1. **How we teach spiritual disciplines and practices.** Most people operating out of The Human Paradigm will ultimately avoid spiritual disciplines and practices (not to mention leave the

church) because they resent them. Still, we're not calling leaders to soften the call to spiritual practices—far from it.

Instead, we have to make sure people are being oriented out of The Human Paradigm and into Jesus' way of approaching spiritual disciplines. We're confident that when Jesus "often withdrew to solitary places to pray"—while there was necessary discipline to overcome his exhaustion and still make space for prayer—there was no drudgery in it. No doubt Jesus approached connecting with the Father and becoming more aware of the Father's nearness and goodness as a delight. It was a meal to be enjoyed, not mush to be endured.

From this place, he was empowered to live a life of care and compassion for others. If, unlike Jesus, we have a root belief that we have to earn God's favor, we will resent both God and the things that we believe we have to do in order to get close to him—and we will rarely see our lives as an instrument of God's grace for others.

I (Brandon) grew up in the South, where there was a huge focus not just on quiet times, as I mentioned above, but also on reading Scripture. I liked the idea of reading the Bible and being quiet before God. Yet I grew tired of trying to read it out of obligation. And I watched most everyone around me struggle to read Scripture with any consistency, as important as we were told it was. To this day, I find that if I'm approaching spiritual practices as tasks to check off because I *should* do them, there's no life in it. Asking, "How am I doing?" by itself just has no horsepower.

But—oh, the glorious "but"—if I'm asking the questions, "Jesus, how can you be this good?" and "How am I doing loving others?" then everything changes. What emerges is a completely different approach to spiritual practices: we practice the disciplines not to earn something but to become fully aware of how our lives can be energized to live in awe of God's goodness and empowered for loving others. This is part of how we "grow in grace" (2 Pet. 3:18).

What we find as we become aware of grace is that everything becomes a response to Jesus, not simply an attempt to be rewarded by him. We don't come to Scripture because we must read our Bible to grow close to Jesus; we read our Bible to become more aware of how Jesus has already brought us close to him and how we can be empowered by him to live lives that bring hope and blessing to others. It's not about earning a reward; it's about responding to a gift that has been given. In this way, The Human Paradigm is interrupted, and all of the disciplines we practice become "get tos," not "have tos." We find ourselves actually wanting to spend time with God, who is so generous to have invited us with lavish love to join him.

For example, not long ago, I (Bill) remember when my wife, Jane, was spending a few days out of town taking care of the grandsons. I called her to see when she was coming home. She informed me that she was staying longer than expected and that she had made additional commitments for the next week. I began to question her and communicate that I was very unhappy with her decision. She had made that decision without talking to me and considering my needs and work that needed to be done at home.

Later, I began to talk to myself: *Bill,* I said, *Jane has supported you and let you be you for forty-six years, and she has never complained when you made commitments without talking to her first to speak, go to meetings, or even play golf with friends.*

I wasn't finished talking to myself, so I went on: *Taking care of people is what Jane does. There is a reason everyone loves her: because she loves them! She serves many, but she serves you the best. So stop trying to stop her from loving others as Christ loved others.*

Now, this could have been the Holy Spirit speaking because I am rarely that brilliant. So I had to repent. In fact, I had to ask a question: "Lord, what do I need to do to love Jane with your love?" The answer came quickly: that I would need to pray and meditate on Scripture. I would also need to serve her and help her with her work so that she could thrive in her ministry to others.

As a result, I went to the spiritual disciplines as I meditated on Scripture and prayed to God. Through these, I discovered in a deeper way what I was beginning to realize: that God wants me to lay down my desires. I was reminded of God's sacrificial love in Jesus to lay down his life and agenda for us, and that reminder triggered obedience in me.

You see what happened? I realized by my experience with God in that moment that I needed to practice certain spiritual disciplines to reorient myself around God and become the kind of person that loves as Christ loved, so that I could live for others. I wanted to know: What was Jane thinking or feeling when she makes decisions? Where does her joy come from? I found that meditating on episodes of Jesus' life and asking him in prayer to help me understand his heart would get me closer to what I saw in Jane.

Once we realize that discipleship is being like Christ, and that doing what he did always leads to loving others and serving them, there is such joy and satisfaction that we can never go back to The Human Paradigm. We forget self, and when we do, our self gets better. This is God's secret sauce. Transformation of the self happens when we're learning to forego the demands of self. The self, paradoxically, is transformed when we focus on others, not on ourselves!

As leaders, therefore, we must teach those in our sphere of influence an approach to disciplines grounded in the questions, "God, how can you be this good?" and "How am I doing with loving others?" We must teach them that they have already been brought close to Jesus, and they just need to become aware of this reality.

2. ***How we approach corporate church services and gatherings.*** I (Bill) recently taught in Brandon's church community in Long Beach, California. At the end of the message, I turned to the congregation and asked the people, "Okay, so . . . what are

you planning on doing with this message? How will your hearing of this message affect those in your life?"

The questions I asked are brilliant questions (ones I learned from others) because just by asking them, you interrupt the consumerist mindset that society and, sadly, the church have conditioned people to follow.

When we gather, we must teach those who are in Christ that they are already close to Jesus. That can sound crazy, especially when we consider the struggle and brokenness of ourselves and the people around us. But in acknowledging this weakness, we can teach what the Bible teaches: despite your brokenness, despite your woundedness, no matter how damaged you may feel, God has brought you close! You don't have to work to get close to him; *you are close* to him. Now to become aware of this reality, that is the thing. As Scripture says, "Draw near to God and he will draw near to you" (James 4:8, ESV). James is not saying that God's nearness is conditional on our posture toward him. Rather, when we respond to God's nearness, he is waiting to make us fully aware of just how near he has brought us.

How to teach this radical message of costly grace is the topic of another, longer book by someone more gifted than the two of us, but suffice it to say, we have to actually teach what Paul taught: that we are already dead, buried, and resurrected with Christ (Col 2:20; 3:1). We work out our wholeness from that place of already being brought near rather than laboring under The Human

Paradigm's false promise of arrival and "being fixed" if we just try hard enough.

Then we are positioned to challenge people, as I did at Brandon's church. We are positioned to truly call people to the depth of a discipleship which costs us everything and which demands not just our efforts but also our very lives. When we truly teach love and grace, we can truly teach the call to discipleship.

3. *How we think about and celebrate "mission."* Further, when we gather, including and especially during Sunday and large church gatherings, we create church culture based on what we celebrate and the questions we ask. And we need to make it clear to people through these activities that discipleship is, in the end, about loving and serving others.

The challenge here is that too many times "mission" and "loving others" are presented as programs or activities (projects), like going to the homeless shelter once a month. We support going to homeless shelters, but we're saying here that as leaders, we have to break down people's notion that mission is confined to a specific slice of the calendar rather than a lifestyle that we engage in at every moment as we become aware of where Jesus is at work around us. When Jesus encountered the woman at Jacob's well in John 4, he didn't look at his sundial and say, "Yes, it's time for my missional hour." No, Jesus was aware that at any moment he might walk into a space where his Father was clearly at work.

How, then, do we lead people from the notion of mission as an event into this awareness of ministry at any possible moment?

As an example, I (Brandon) have begun to close our worship gatherings for our church by asking, "How are you doing loving those that Jesus has placed in your life?" and "What is Jesus speaking to you?" and "How will you respond this week?"

We have incorporated very specific training to clarify what we mean by "those that Jesus has placed in your life," such as the idea of "people of peace," so it's not quite as broad as it sounds at first (see more on this under point five below about leading discipleship groups). But the point here is that we are being intentional about communicating that discipleship is not a two-hour activity we fit into our already-busy schedules. We are seeking to create a culture based on the core premise that discipleship is about orienting our lives around loving others and being prepared to watch the kingdom of God manifest and to tell the story of God.

4. *How we teach evangelism.* In addition to the challenge of re-teaching people what mission is, we must also shift how we teach people to share God's story for evangelism. Let's face it, many people have wonky paradigms for what evangelism is because of The Human Paradigm. They have been taught that you're "doing evangelism right" if you're trying to persuade someone within an apologetics argument, or you're angling for an opportunity to share Jesus with them. If you do it the "right way," you'll convince people to become a Christian. Apologetics are

great, and so is being prepared to share the hope that lives within us (1 Pet. 3:15), but if those things are not born out of Christlike presence with others and out of an experience of love, they will have little effect and value. We need to train people to be good neighbors. We need to teach hospitality and listening. And how to ask good questions. We need to teach people that being present with others is at the heart of evangelism. Again, that's the subject of a different book, but suffice it to say that re-teaching and re-training people how to live their lives with and for others—ready to explain the hope that comes from Jesus—is a major challenge.

First things first, though: Are we creating cultures based on The Human Paradigm of "How are you doing?" or are we orienting people into the bigger questions of "God, how can you be this good?" and "How am I doing loving others?"

If we ask these questions, we can start to understand how to create a culture of discipleship in our unique contexts.

5. ***How we lead discipleship groups.*** Discipleship groups will not thrive or reproduce if they're based solely on reading Scripture and sharing in some sort of openness and accountability. As great as those things are, if they lack the intentionality of challenging people to focus their love—expressed in action—on others, there will be no movement. In fact, groups that are built on such principles often become exclusionary. Discipleship groups should include Bible study, vulnerability, and accountability, but the context—the container in which these things make sense and

find their bearing—has to be clearly set. The big context of discipleship is mission. Grounded in God's love, we are called to focus our lives on loving others. Thus, the end point of discipleship is loving others.

The trickiness in this is, again, how we do it. Many people, when thinking about "mission," have vague notions of mission as going down to the soup kitchen, going on an international trip, or angling for an opportunity to tell someone about Jesus. There's a lot of demystifying that has to happen, and the key to making discipleship work is to make it concrete and practical, as Jesus always did. Notice how often Jesus gets really concrete with his disciples: *Give the people something to eat. Sell what you have and give to the poor. Go to your brother who is offended by you.* Love expressed as action—not just sweeping theological statements—is where Jesus usually lands.

So if the end goal is loving others, how do we form discipleship processes based on practical ways of loving and serving others?

Asking the Three Questions

As an example, in my (Brandon's) community, we have launched discipleship groups of three to six people that meet weekly (at least) and journey together for more than a year. Each meeting has a basic, though very flexible, outline. We share it with you so that you can adopt and even adapt it for your own context. The order of the first two is interchangeable, but it goes like this:

1. ***The First Question.*** We start each group by asking the question, "How are you experiencing God's goodness?" This provides space to keep people grounded in an awareness of God's love, grace, and provision. It's a way of considering God's nearness, even in the midst of great challenges. If people are willing to be open and honest about their soul and the suffering they might be walking through, the results can be connectedness and empathy and a mutual sharing of one another's burdens.

2. ***The Second Question.*** Next, we ask, "How's it going with loving the people Jesus has given you to love?" We have very specific categories for these groups, including loved ones (that is, family and friends), spiritual family (that is, our brothers and sisters in Christ), and our neighbors (that is, those around us).

   We also use the "person of peace" concept to help clarify how we can be aware of where Jesus is clearly at work among our neighbors who don't identify with Jesus.[9] By asking this question, we interrupt the gravitational pull back toward living only in the, "How am I doing?" question. In fact, more specifically, we focus our discipleship efforts on what it looks like to love our neighbors and finding persons of peace because there's always a gravitational pull in human hearts to focus on loving only our family and spiritual family—those people who are often most like us—and avoid our neighbors, or neglect to reorient our lives to be with and for them.

The Place of Obedience

We find that asking "How's it going with loving others?" tends to surface any discipleship issue that needs to be addressed. If, for example, someone is running around working eighty hours a week with no time to be with their neighbors or the persons of peace in their life, that will immediately surface. If someone is struggling with hidden sin, they won't have a lot of energy left over to be with others. Asking the question, "How are you doing loving others?" is the best question for spiritual transformation that lines us up with the mission and heart of Jesus.

3. **The Third Question.** The question with which we end our time together in discipleship groups is simply, "What is Jesus speaking to you, and how will you respond this week?" By asking this question with two parts, we place a value on action that goes beyond mere reflection. We coach people toward specificity so that responding in the week ahead is clear and specific, not vague or ambiguous.

The goal in our discipleship process is to deconstruct The Human Paradigm, with its focus on arriving, and to replace it with three discipleship pictures:

ADOPTION!   AMBASSADOR   ABUNDANT LIFE

Christlike disciples are grounded in their *adoption*. In response to the grace of God, they ask, "How can you be this good, God?" They are constantly learning to surrender their experience of shame to the reality of God's all-embracing love. They are constantly checking in, with gratitude, on how they are experiencing God's provision and goodness, even in the midst of suffering.

Disciples live as *ambassadors* of the kingdom of heaven. They focus on loving those Jesus has given them by asking, "How am I doing with loving the people Jesus has given me to love?" They are committed to making present the kingdom of God where they live, work, and play, knowing they share in Jesus' work of seeing all things "made new" (Rev. 21:5).

Disciples live the *abundant life* by listening and responding to Jesus and asking, "Jesus, what are you speaking to me?" Then they respond, getting very specific about what tangible action they are called to take—be it specific spiritual disciplines or some sort of risk that will require them to trust God in a deeper way. They ask this question and respond, not from The Human Paradigm with its focus on *how I'm doing* and trying to earn something. They respond, instead, from The Jesus Paradigm, in light of Jesus' grace and love, and they do this with obedience in their heart, soul, and conscience.

These three pictures are about growing awareness and abiding in Jesus. In addition to asking these questions, we use materials that center on spiritual practices in three categories—what we call

The Slow Life, The Grounded Life, The Generous Life—which are meant to develop awareness of Jesus' nearness and goodness and our adoption in him. In fact, we've put these materials into book form.[10] But we are very clear that the curriculum is *not* the resources we use; rather, the curriculum is the actual act of responding to the questions. We like to call our response to God the "Big Curriculum" because the "Big Curriculum" is everyday life itself. Discipleship comes when we reorient our lives around being present with others. In our experience, asking the last two questions about loving others, in the context of abiding in our adoption as sons and daughters of God, creates the best context for transformation and discipleship that we have found.

Asking these three questions are the beginning steps for many, but they are significant. The important thing is that you, as leader, can change the way people approach discipleship, and you can help catalyze a new movement of disciple-making in your context.

But wait! You, dear reader, will need to do this yourself! Start by asking yourself these questions. It takes time and effort to practice these questions, but when we practice them, they can become habits; habits become our character. Asking these questions helps transform us, and this ongoing transformation capacitates us to become disciple makers as we learn to lead others through the questions. But we cannot lead others into questions we have not asked ourselves.

Ask the Right Questions *to Yourself*

1. *God, how can you be this good, to adopt me when I'm still unsorted?* Practice the discipline of consciously receiving the new identity that comes from adoption. This may not come naturally to you, and you might need to really practice it! But by practicing, we can start doing away with the belief that we have to earn something to be "in."
2. *How am I doing loving the people whom God has placed in my life?* What do you notice? What thoughts come up when you consider this question? Where is Jesus out ahead of you, having prepared good works in advance, that you should walk in them like Ephesians 2:8-9 describes? Where and how, this week, is Jesus calling you to love your friends and neighbors in concrete, practical terms?
3. *Jesus, what are you speaking to me through your Holy Spirit?* Learn to discern how you hear the leading of the Holy Spirit, as you read Scripture and as you listen for his whisper in everyday life. Try to make your response as concrete as possible. If, for example, you sense a need for more rest and greater margin in your life, don't just say, "I'm going to live slower," but rather, "I'm going to take three slow, prayerful walks around my neighborhood this week." The more specific and concrete, the more helpful it is!

These questions can become a daily practice that helps us stay grounded in our lives as disciples—adopted in love, called as ambassadors, and filled with the Holy Spirit as we listen and respond.

Toward the Future of the Church

Our goal is to help you move out of The Human Paradigm, with its tantalizing but impossible promise of arrival, into abiding in Christ and learning to orient your life around others. This is urgent work.

The contemporary world is asking an ancient and poetic question: "Is there healing balm in Gilead?" The person on the street wants something real, something that works, something to bind up their wounds and give them relief. And the false promise of discipleship has not delivered. They try church, they hang out with our disciples, and they have largely concluded, "No, there is no healing balm in the church."

The sad result is a growing number of "nones" and "dones." "Nones" are those people who profess no religious affiliation or belief system, and "dones" are those people who have tried religion but are now done with it.[11] We believe the "nones" and "dones" derive greatly from the fact that the church has not delivered Christlike disciples to the world.

The true promise of discipleship comes from a wholly different paradigm, one that can deliver on hope, one that can create a true movement of discipleship in the church, even as the church we know fades away.

The true promise is hope and life and love in Christ.

Rather than panicking or trying to throw better parties in our churches, we have the exciting opportunity to rediscover, redefine, and recreate what the church is! The church can be a vibrant, dynamic, life-saving body of passionate disciples who make disciples. We have an opportunity to rediscover the church as it existed in the Book of Acts, when by the power of the Holy Spirit, people were added daily to their numbers. We have the opportunity to live the great adventure of a life lived for others, with Jesus.

Here's to the journey that awaits us!

NOTES

1. "Why the Missional Movement Will Fail (Pt 2)," *Verge*, accessed March 27, 2019, http://www.vergenetwork. org/2011/09/21/mike-breen-why-the-missional-movement-will-fail-part-2/.
2. See Isaiah 58 as a whole, especially verse 8.
3. From notes, Dallas Willard lecture, Long Beach, California, June 31, 2011.
4. Dallas Willard, *The Great Omission: Reclaiming Jesus' Essential Teachings on Discipleship* (New York: HarperCollins, 2014), 34.
5. 2 Peter 3:18. See also Paul's prayers for the church in Ephesians 3:14-21.
6. Dallas Willard, *The Divine Conspiracy: Rediscovering Our Hidden Life in God* (San Francisco: HarperCollins, 1998), 41.
7. C.S. Lewis, *Mere Christianity* (New York: HarperOne, 2015), 205.

8. Dietrich Bonhoeffer, *Letters and Papers From Prison*, Dietrich Bonhoeffer Works, vol. 8 (Minneapolis: Fortress Press, 2010), 27.
9. Our friend Alex Absalom explores the concept of the "person of peace" in detail in his free eBook, *The Viral Gospel*, available through www.exponential.org/resource-ebooks/the-viral-gospel/.
10. You can get this material in Brandon Cook's *Learning to Live and Love Like Jesus* (2018).
11. "Nones" are those people who profess no religious affiliation or belief system; see Becka A. Alper, "Why America's 'nones' don't identify with a religion," Pew Research Center, August 8, 2018, www.pewresearch.org/fact-tank/2018/08/08/why-americas-nones-dont-identify-with-a-religion/. "Dones" are those who have tried religion and are now done with it; see "America's Changing Religious Landscape," Pew Research Center, May 12, 2015, www.pewforum.org/2015/05/12/americas-changing-religious-landscape/.

ABOUT THE AUTHORS

BILL HULL is a discipleship evangelist. His passion is to help the church return to its disciple-making roots. This God-given desire has manifested itself in 20 years of serving in pastoral service and authoring 25 books, including *Jesus Christ Disciplemaker*, *The Disciple-Making Pastor*, and *The Disciple-Making Church*. Bill speaks about discipleship around the world to both congregations and leaders. He is also a co-founder of The Bonhoeffer Project (www.thebonhoefferproject.com), a group of nationally known thought leaders championing a "new" gospel—that which Jesus taught—saying that those who are called to salvation are called to discipleship. Bill and his wife, Jane, make their home in Long Beach, California, and are the parents of two grown sons. More about Bill can be found at www.billhull.net.

BRANDON COOK serves as lead pastor at Long Beach Christian Fellowship and is a co-founder of The Bonhoeffer Project. He is also an apprentice trainer with Reinvent Ministries (www.reinventministries.org) and co-host of The Desire Line Podcast (www.desirelinepodcast.com). Originally from Birmingham, Alabama, Brandon has studied at Wheaton College, Jerusalem University College, Brandeis University, and The Oxford

Centre for Hebrew and Jewish Studies. He lives in Long Beach, California, with his wife, Rebecca, and their three children. Follow his photography on Instagram at @brandonalancook and read his poetry and other writings at www.storyflight.com.

Become a Disciple-Making Leader

the BONHOEFFER project

A year-long leadership development community

RECLAIM THE DISCIPLESHIP-FIRST GOSPEL
CRAFT YOUR DISCIPLE-MAKING PLAN
CHANGE THE WORLD

JOIN A COHORT
WWW.THEBONHOEFFERPROJECT.COM

PUBLISHED BY

TRUSTED DISCIPLESHIP RESOURCES

Grow as a Person

Resource Your Group

Enjoy the Process

Learn from authors like Jim Putman, Bill Hull, John Mark Hicks, Dave Clayton, *and more* . . .

Subscribe at www.himpublications.com

BUY FOR YOUR GROUP

Get *The False Promise of Discipleship* from

HIMPUBLICATIONS.COM

Rescue discipleship from the American gospel by learning to ask the right questions.

- → Embrace Jesus-style discipleship by asking the right questions
- → Learn practical ways to train small group leaders at your church how to focus on God and loving others
- → Get your whole church to make disciples with the right discipleship questions—so they can truly grow

Printed by Libri Plureos GmbH in Hamburg, Germany